Out of
CONTROL
The Science of **Wildfires**

by Lyn A. Sirota

Content Adviser:
David R. Weise, Ph.D., Supervisory Research Forester,
U.S. Forest Service, Pacific Southwest Research Station,
Forest Fire Laboratory

Science Adviser:
Terrence E. Young Jr., M.Ed., M.L.S.,
Jefferson Parish (Louisiana) Public School System

Reading Adviser:
Rosemary G. Palmer, Ph.D., Department of Literacy,
College of Education, Boise State University

Compass Point Books • 151 Good Counsel Drive, P. O. Box 669 • Mankato, MN 56002-0669

This book was manufactured with paper containing
at least 10 percent post-consumer waste.

Library of Congress Cataloging-in-Publication Data
Sirota, Lyn A., 1963–
   Out of control : the science of wildfires / by Lyn A. Sirota.
       p. cm.—(Headline Science)
   Includes bibliographical references and index.
   ISBN 978-0-7565-4064-7 (library binding)
1. Wildfires—Juvenile literature. 2. Wildfires—Prevention and control—Juvenile literature.
I. Title.
   SD421.23.S58 2009
   634.9'618—dc22   2008038377

Editor: Anthony Wacholtz
Designer: Ellen Schofield and Ashlee Suker
Page Production: Ashlee Suker
Photo Researcher: Eric Gohl

Art Director: LuAnn Ascheman-Adams
Creative Director: Joe Ewest
Editorial Director: Nick Healy
Managing Editor: Catherine Neitge

Photographs ©: Shari L. Morris/Art Life Images, cover (bottom); fabphoto/iStockphoto, cover (inset, left), 29;
Konstantin Mironov/Shutterstock, cover (inset, middle), 9, 11; Dhoxax/Shutterstock, cover (inset, right), 10; Mark
O. Thiessen/National Geographic/Getty Images, 5; Bettmann/Corbis, 8; Arnold John Labrentz/Shutterstock, 12;
Wikipedia, public-domain image, 13; AP Images/Mike Meadows, 15; Scott Vickers/iStockphoto, 16; David McNew/
Getty Images, 17, 20; George Frey/AFP/Getty Images, 18; Mike Norton/Shutterstock, 21; Krista Banks/iStockphoto,
23; David Goddard/Getty Images, 24; David Hancock/AFP/Getty Images, 25; Tim Matsui/Liaison/Getty Images,
27; AP Images/Ben Margot, 30 (top); Justin Sullivan/Getty Images, 30 (bottom); Jeff T. Green/Getty Images, 31; AP
Images/Joerg Sarbach, 32; University Corporation for Atmospheric Research/Photo by Herb Stein, 35; NOAA/OSEI,
37; AP Images/Cheryl Hatch, Pool, 39; Louisa Gouliamaki/AFP/Getty Images, 41; AP Images/Marcio Jose Sanchez,
42; Kevin Moloney/Getty Images, 43.

Visit Compass Point Books on the Internet at www.compasspointbooks.com
or e-mail your request to custserv@compasspointbooks.com

Chapter 1

Forests
Under Fire
Page 4

Chapter 3

After the Burn
Page 19

Chapter 5

High-tech
Blaze Blasting
Page 34

Chapter 2

The Fire
Environment
Page 14

Chapter 4

Combating
the Fire
Page 26

Timeline   Page 44
Glossary   Page 45
Further Resources   Page 46
Source Notes   Page 47
Index   Page 48

THE AGE OF MEGA-FIRES

>>> CBS News
December 30, 2007

This past fall, wildfires ripped through Southern California, burning more than 500,000 acres (200,000 hectares) of trees, destroying over 2,000 homes, and claiming nine lives. Scientists now say we should brace ourselves for more and more of these fires in the coming years, because there's been an enormous change in Western fires. In truth, we've never seen anything like them in recorded history.

It appears we're living in a new age of mega-fires—forest infernos ten times bigger than the fires we're used to seeing.

Wildfires that take place in wilderness or rural areas are devastating. They sweep through Montana forests. They roar through southern California brush. Wildfires race across Nebraska prairies, jump around in the wetlands of Florida, and burn for months in the tundra of Alaska. Wildfires burn grass, shrubs, and trees, and it often takes years for the trees and shrubs to grow back. These blazes can move up to 14 miles (22.4 kilometers) per hour.

In 2007 alone, nearly 86,000 rural and wilderness wildfires burned more than 9 million acres (3.6 million hectares) of land. More than $1.8 billion

The number of acres burned from wildfires in the United States has nearly doubled in recent years.

KEEPING CURRENT

News changes every minute, and readers need access to the latest information to keep current. Here are a few key search terms to help you locate up-to-the-minute wildfire headlines:

American Red Cross wildfires

FEMA wildfires

GeoMAC wildfire viewer

National Interagency Fire Center

U.S. Fire Administration

U.S. Forest Service

USGS wildfires

wildfire maps

was spent to contain those wildland fires. The human cost was high as well. In 2006 and 2007, 33 wildland firefighters were killed. During the 1990s, the death toll reached 133.

THE FIRE TRIANGLE

No matter where it starts, a wildfire needs three things to burn: heat, fuel, and oxygen. These three things work together to create a fire and keep it going. Heat is necessary to start combustion—the chemical reaction that combines the fuel and oxygen. This chemical reaction produces heat (a flame), which can keep the fire going. The flame heats the unburned fuel such as leaves, branches, grasses, shrubs, and trees. The transfer of heat enables a fire to grow. The heat causes the water in the fuel to evaporate, which makes it easier for the fire to spread. The speed of heat transfer plays an important role in the behavior of wildfires.

U.S. WILDLAND FIRES AND ACRES BURNED

Year	Number of Fires	Acres Burned
2007	85,705	9,328,045
2000	92,250	7,393,493
1990	66,841	4,621,621
1980	234,892	5,260,825
1970	121,736	3,278,565
1960	103,387	4,478,188

Source: National Interagency Fire Center

HEADLINE SCIENCE

All three sides of the fire triangle—fuel, air (oxygen), and heat—are needed to start a fire.

Heat transfers three ways in wildfires—through convection, radiation, and conduction. Convection occurs through the flow of liquids or gases moving around burned fuels. Convection in the atmosphere causes cumulonimbus (thunderstorm) clouds to grow bigger. Flames—which are hot gases that glow—flow around unburned fuels, and heat is transferred by convection to the fuel. For example, when you boil corn in hot water, the hot water transfers heat to the cooler ear of corn by convection.

Radiation happens through rays of sun or a flame. The sun transfers heat through space to Earth by radiation. Radiation from a flame is mostly responsible for preheating the unburned fuels before the flame gets to the fuel. Radiation and convection transfer more heat to fuels than conduction.

Heat transfers by conduction through the movement of molecules within a solid fuel or between two objects by direct contact. For example, conduction occurs when your finger heats up by touching the side of a hot pan. Conduction also transfers heat from the outside of a solid object to its inside. Conduction is not the primary way that heat transfers in a wildland fire because wood is not an effective heat conductor—heat does not pass through wood easily.

A fuel is anything that combusts, or is able to ignite and burn. The size, shape, quantity, moisture content, and arrangement of these fuels determine the burning rate and the spread rate. Wildfires burn live plants and dead ones. Dead fuels (wood, grass, or leaves) are like sponges and don't actively control how much water they contain. They absorb water from the atmosphere, but they also lose water

< BLAZING HISTORY >

One of the worst wildfires in U.S. history was the Peshtigo fire, which burned 1.5 million acres (600,000 hectares) of forestland in Wisconsin and Michigan. The October 8, 1871, fire killed between 1,200 and 2,400 people. The Great Chicago Fire burned on the same day 250 miles (400 km) away.

Another terrible wildfire in the United States happened during the summer of 1988 at Yellowstone National Park in Wyoming. For months the weather had been hot and dry. On the worst single day, August 20, tremendous winds pushed fire across more than 150,000 acres (60,000 hectares). Some park facilities and roads closed to the public, and residents of nearby towns outside of the park feared for their property and their lives.

to it. Live plants control their water because they need water to live.

For dead fuels, the size and shape of the fuel help determine how easily it absorbs and loses water. Grass, leaves, and pine needles—also called fine fuels—are usually drier when they are dead and can quickly dry out. They also burn quickly because they can heat up fast. Tree branches, logs, and trunks take longer to catch fire and burn. In areas with lots of fine fuels, less energy is needed from the fire to keep it going. In areas with bigger fuels, the fire must produce more energy to heat up the fuels in order to keep spreading.

Oxygen, the third piece of the fire triangle, is an important part of any fire. When fuel burns, it reacts with oxygen in the air, which releases heat (energy) and produces smoke (carbon dioxide, water vapor, and unburned particles). The chemical reaction in a wildfire is the same reaction that a plant uses to make its food, but reversed. A green plant uses the sun's energy to combine carbon dioxide and water to make plant parts.

Fuels—such as twigs and leaves—on the forest floor allow wildfires to spread quickly from tree to tree.

WHAT CAUSES WILDFIRES?

Although people start four out of five wildfires, many begin naturally from lightning strikes. Lack of rain increases the possibility of wildfires breaking out because the fuels dry out. In fact, many wildfires are reported during an area's dry season. Fires can also begin as a result of volcanic activity. Lava flows down the side of a volcano, igniting everything in its path.

Humans start wildfires carelessly or intentionally. Wildfires can start

Areas with heavy vegetation, such as the grasslands of South Africa, are at a higher risk for wildfires.

from campfires, cigarettes or matches tossed into dry grass, and sparks from burning trash piles. Sparks from trains, electrical power lines, and off-road vehicles, such as motorcycles and all-terrain vehicles, may start a wildfire. Anything that can make a spark may lead to a fire.

There are three classes of wildfires: surface, ground, and crown. A fire's class is determined by the type of fuel involved and the intensity of the fire.

A surface fire is the most common type of fire. It burns slowly along the forest floor. A surface fire can burn, damage, or kill trees and shrubs. Surface fires with small flames usually present little danger to large, mature trees and root systems if there isn't too much fuel on the ground by the trees.

A ground fire is the most difficult type of fire to see. It burns

out of sight underground through fuels on the forest floor or in organic soils. It can burn through the roots of trees.

Low-intensity surface fires creep slowly along the ground and consume all of the smaller fuels in their paths.

Ground fires are dangerous because they can't be easily detected and can erupt into surface fires.

Crown fires are generally a result of a surface fire that has spread vertically into the crowns (shrubs) and canopy (trees). They can spread rapidly by wind and are the most violent of the wildfire classes. They can lift firebrands—pieces of burning wood—high in the atmosphere. These firebrands can cause other fires to start far away from the main fire. In Australia, burning bark from a eucalyptus tree was transported 18 miles (30 km) during a large crown fire. Crown fires are dangerous and difficult to control.

The types of plants that grow in a particular area can affect the spread

Crown fires can consume entire forests because the flames spread through the air and can easily jump from one tree to another.

< FIRE CLOUDS >

Large fires create their own clouds called pyrocumulus, which are similar to thunderstorm clouds. The water released by burning rises above the fire and condenses into clouds at the top of the smoke column above the fire. The clouds can even produce rain. Most rainfall from a pyro-thunderstorm evaporates quickly in the dry air above the fire zone and doesn't reach the ground. Strong winds can come from the clouds, causing dangerous and unpredictable fire conditions.

of wildfires because the shape and size of the fuel affect how it burns. Trees and shrubs have various leaf shapes, branch sizes, and heights. Pine trees, for example, can burn more rapidly than maple trees because of the shape of their leaves. The leaves of some trees and shrubs contain chemicals such as resin and waxes, which give off more heat when they burn, helping the fire to spread faster.

Rising temperatures and global warming also contribute to wildfires. "Climate change in the West is a reality," says Thomas Swetnam of the University of Arizona in Tucson. "Now, we're starting to see the effects." Earlier spring snowmelts create longer fire seasons, and this accounts for the trend, he says. Swetnam reported in a 2006 study published in the journal *Science* that the number of large wildfires (greater than 1,000 acres or 400 hectares) in Western forests greatly increased in the mid-1980s. The average length of the fire season between 1987 and 2003 was 78 days longer than it was between 1970 and 1986—a 64 percent increase.

BLAZED AND CONFUSED.

The New York Times
November 3, 2007

In the last century, a greater proportion of Southern California has burned than that of any other part of the country. Chaparral shrublands—not forest—cover much of our landscape and account for the vast majority of what burns. The United States Forest Service, which devotes more than half of its budget to fire-related activities, spends most of that money to protect residences built in these shrublands.

Yet we have just seen, for the second time in less than a decade, wind-driven fires causing at least $1 billion in damage. The magnitude of these events makes it clear that it is time to re-evaluate the wildfire problem and how we deal with it as a matter of public policy. There is much confusion over the causes and behavior of these fires.

Fire whirls caused by strong winds can rip trees out by their roots. These tornadoes of flame form when strong winds create an eddy, or a circular movement. They are rare, but they can be extremely dangerous. Strong winds can intensify an already raging fire and play a large role in the spread of wildfires.

There are three main factors that affect how a wildfire will burn. This fire environment triangle incudes air mass (with its wind, temperature, and humidity), fuels, and topography.

AIR MASS

Strong winds push flames toward new fuel sources. Wind picks up and transfers burning embers, sparks, and other material that can catch fire.

Wind provides oxygen to the fire. Blowing wind can also dry the moist areas. This allows the fire to maintain itself. Wildfires can also generate their own wind. The air above the hot

flames becomes heated, causing it to rise. This movement allows fresh air and a supply of oxygen to keep the fire burning.

The temperature in the burn zone affects how quickly a fire can start and

A fire whirl in Ventura, California, was fueled by a wildfire that lasted more than three weeks.

Wildfires descended upon Santiago Canyon, California, in October 2007, burning approximately 28,000 acres (11,200 hectares) of land and destroying 15 houses.

burn. Fires in shade do not burn as quickly as fires in sunlight. Fuels are warmer on hot days and can start burning more quickly than cold fuels. Higher temperatures also cause dead fuels to lose more moisture and dry out.

The level of humidity, or moisture in the air, can affect the fire because the fuel can absorb the moisture in like a sponge. This slows the spread of flames. Because humidity is usually greater at night, fires burn less intensely and do not spread as far. Firefighters take advantage of this to put out wildfires at night.

FUELS

Once a fire starts, the fuel source allows it to spread and grow. Fuel can be living or dead vegetation, such as twigs, leaves, moss, and lichen. The size of the fuels and how they are distributed across the area help determine where and how fast a fire will burn. Smaller fuels ignite more easily and usually in a shorter time than larger fuels. That is why kindling (small pieces of wood) is used instead of big logs to start a fire.

If the fuel occurs in patches instead of like a carpet, a fire will have a harder time spreading horizontally. If fuels are arranged vertically, a fire can spread from the ground into the tops of trees, causing a crown fire. The fuel is described by the moisture content and its size and shape. The higher the moisture content, the slower the burning process.

TOPOGRAPHY

The topography, or shape of the land, also affects the spread of fire. Topography includes slope, elevation, and aspect. Slope measures how steep the land is. The steeper the land, the faster a fire can spread upward. Fire spreads faster up a slope than it spreads

down a slope. The hot gases from the fire rise quickly and "preheat" the higher land.

The elevation of the land—how high it is above sea level—influences the air's temperature and humidity. The temperature and humidity determine what kind of plants will grow there and how wet the fuels are.

Slope aspect is the direction that a hill faces. Aspect also influences what

Firefighters and crew members from the California Department of Forestry attempt to contain a wildfire burning down a steep hill.

In Show Low, Arizona, a single road contained a wildfire that had consumed 500 square miles (1,300 square km) of land. The road cut off the wildfire from any additional fuel sources.

kinds of plants will grow. In the United States, southern and southwestern aspects receive more sunlight, which makes them drier and warmer than northern and northeastern aspects. Moss grows on the north side of a tree because it is usually cooler and moister than the south side.

Every fire is different in the way it behaves because of slope, elevation, and aspect, but the land is the one thing that remains the same. It can allow firefighters to predict how the fire will behave in a specific area. Some land has barriers such as rocks, boulders, and bodies of water that will not allow fires to spread quickly.

Many things affect whether a fire creeps across the forest floor in a ground fire or advances from treetop to treetop in a crown fire. Predicting the movement of a fire requires the knowledge of many disciplines, such as chemistry, physics, geology, meteorology, and ecology.

WILDFIRES LEAVE BEHIND MORE THAN ASHES.

Science Daily
October 8, 2007

The recent wildfires raging throughout the Southern California region have already caused plenty of devastation, leaving lost lives, charred homes, property destroyed and families displaced.

But what people may not know is that the wildfires are also causing damage on an "elemental" level—that is, in increased amounts of elements such as iron, aluminum and mercury accumulating in watershed systems after a fire. Enhanced concentrations of such elements in stream water adversely affect the quality of downstream water supplies and the rate of vegetation regrowth.

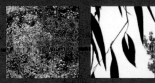

A Ash from wildfires in southern California's neighborhoods poses a serious threat to people and ecosystems. According to one federal study, wildfires that burned in residential areas created ash with high levels of arsenic, lead, and other toxic metals. Rainstorms can wash dangerous substances into waterways, which pollute streams and threaten wildlife.

When wood burns, ash is left over. Water from soil collected under the ash in this study was as strong as ammonia (a mild cleaner). At other places, the water from the soil was nearly as corrosive as lye (a strong cleaner), which can be harmful to the environment. Metals, particularly arsenic, in the ash were found in higher concentrations than would

In May 2007, large wildfires left layers of ash that covered the hills overlooking downtown Los Angeles. Because it can be easily transported by the wind, the ash posed a potential threat to the city.

be allowed by federal standards for cleaning up hazardous waste sites. Ash from nonresidential areas burned by the same fires was not as hazardous because there were no metals like arsenic and lead.

According to research by scientists at the National Center for Atmospheric Research and the University of Colorado in Boulder, large fires can release as much carbon dioxide into the air in a few weeks as the state's entire motor vehicle traffic does in a year. Even though large fires can release a lot of carbon dioxide in a short time, scientists have estimated that wildfires produce only about 5 percent of the emissions produced by automobiles in the United States in a year. Carbon dioxide emissions present a challenge because of their link to greenhouse gases and global warming. Plants usually regrow in areas burned by wildfires, and they capture the carbon dioxide back from the atmosphere.

Smoke is a product of wildfires It affects the quality of the air. The smoke itself is a mixture of gases and fine particles from burning trees and other plant materials. Smoke can hurt the eyes, irritate the respiratory system, and worsen chronic heart and lung diseases. It can cause coughing,

Large clouds of smoke billowed from the massive wildfires in Oregon's Wallowa Whitman National Forest.

a scratchy throat, sinus irritation, shortness of breath, chest pains, headaches, stinging eyes, runny noses, and asthma flare-ups. Smoke from fires in polluted areas can also contain several other harmful chemicals that aren't found in normal wildfire smoke.

Wildfires themselves create an incredible danger when they spread out of control over large areas. Human and animal lives can be lost, and property damage can run in the millions of dollars. People are injured or killed because they wait too long before evacuating when a wildfire is threatening. Even with modern safety equipment, wildfires still kill firefighters. The flames in a wildfire are about 1,600 to 1,800 degrees Fahrenheit (870 to 1,000 degrees Celsius). In comparison, the broiler of a household oven is about 550 F (290 C).

Fire ecologists say these intense forest fires show that the forests have become "unhealthy." The wildfires that used to naturally pass through these forests were not allowed to burn over the last century. In 1935, the U.S. Forest Service wanted to protect America's wood supply, so it established a rule to put out all fires by 10 A.M. the day after they started. In 1943, a forester named Harold Weaver published evidence explaining the harmful effects of eliminating fire from ponderosa pine forests. Years of scientific research have shown that fire can be beneficial.

POSITIVE OUTCOMES

Fire is a natural part of many ecosystems. Historically, fire burned in most plant communities, and the plants adapted. Many plants and animals rely on fire to create conditions where they like to live and grow. As plants grow, they use the sun's energy to convert carbon dioxide and water into plant parts. The roots absorb nutrients from the soil, which the plant then uses and stores. As plants grow, they drop dead parts (leaves, branches) on the ground. The plants grow larger and become more crowded, which changes the environment for both plants and animals.

Flowers and other plants in a lodgepole pine forest flourish after a wildfire.

HEADLINE SCIENCE

Fire plays many roles in an ecosystem. It releases stored nutrients in plant leaves. It prunes some plants, while it kills others, creating homes for animals. Fire also exposes bare ground for seeds to begin new life.

A lack of fire may be responsible for the increase in numbers of threatened and endangered species in certain ecosystems. The Kirkland's warbler—the rarest warbler in North America—lives in the jack pine forests of Michigan. This bird prefers to nest in the young jack pines that sprout following wildfires. Certain types of plants are seen for only a few years after areas have been hit by a fire. Then they "disappear" until the next fire.

In the past, Native Americans burned areas to make food gathering easier or to make hunting better. Farmers light fires to burn weeds and the remains of some crops after the crops have been harvested. Fires like these are called prescribed, or controlled, burns and are managed so they don't burn out of control.

Prescribed burning is a technique used for several purposes in forest and range management. Fire is commonly used to restore and maintain prairies on the Great Plains. In forests, prescribed burning is used to mimic the natural role of fire. Some types of pine trees have cones that must be heated before the seed will fall out. The tiny seeds of the giant sequoia must begin to grow on bare soil created by burning in order to survive. Other seeds are stored in the soil and only grow after a fire.

Fire also helps to spread seeds. Ashes from the fire put nutrients back into the soil, which makes it better for animals and new plants. Fire burns dead fuels that have accumu-

Prescribed field burning after a harvest has many benefits. The burning controls erosion and destroys weeds and leftover crops, and there is usually a larger harvest the following season.

NOW YOU KNOW

In Arizona, 200 animal species moved to another area because of wildfires. They include Mexican gray wolves, mountain lions, coyotes, weasels, bobcats, snakes, and 162 types of birds.

< FIGHTING FIRE WITH FIRE >

Starting a wildfire can also help stop a wildfire. Firefighters start a backfire, which burns a stretch of land in front of the fire. The backfire consumes all the trees, shrubs, and litter that can fuel the fire. It is a way for the firefighters to slow the spread of the original wildfire. The Forest Service sometimes starts small, controlled fires that burn old, dry undergrowth. This helps prevent future fires by removing the fuel they would need. A fire ecologist must carefully study a wilderness area before deciding whether to set a backfire.

Firemen in Sydney, Australia, created a controlled backfire to protect a house in the path of a wildfire.

lated, which can be hazardous. By killing some trees and shrubs, openings are created in forests that are used by various types of plants, birds, and animals.

Although wildfires can be devastating, they can also benefit ecosystems. Decomposing leaves, branches, and trees in a forest begin to build up. A natural fire has a "cleaning" effect on the forest. It allows more room for plants and trees to grow and spread out. It also clears the way for more sunlight to reach the forest floor. This enables new growth, such as plants and tree sprouts.

Fires remove diseased, insect-infected, or weakened trees and other vegetation. Fire can also act to regulate some insect and disease outbreaks. It limits the amount and spread of certain species that threaten the overall health of the ecosystem. For example, the mountain pine beetle is a serious forest problem. Outbreaks of these insects have killed millions of trees. Fire has helped manage this problem.

ARSON FIRE FORCES HUNDREDS OF HAWAIIANS TO FLEE

>>> MSNBC
October 28, 2007

Brush fires that appeared to be the work of arsonists burned out of control Sunday along the coast of Hawaii's largest island, sending hundreds of people fleeing inland. No homes were damaged and no one was injured, but officials ... worried the fires could approach residential areas ... said Duane Hosaka, staff officer for Hawaii County Civil Defense.

The blazes covered ... more than 3 square miles (7.8 square kilometers), near the northwestern tip of the island and were not contained, Hosaka said. More than 60 fire departments were involved. "It's still burning out of control," Hosaka said. "If they were to go back home and the fire were still burning ... and we had to close the roads, they wouldn't have any way of getting out."

Fighting wildfires requires specially trained teams of firefighters called wildland firefighters. The first attempts to put out a wildfire are called initial attacks. If more firefighters and more time are required, the wildfire is called an extended attack fire.

Firefighters travel to a wildfire in many ways. Smoke jumpers fight wildfires located in places far from people, highways, or roads. Teams of smoke jumpers are flown to the site and parachute or slide down a rope to the wildfire. These trained professionals come from throughout the country to jump out of airplanes and fight wildfires.

Smoke jumpers fight fires in remote locations. There are more than 270 smoke jumpers working for the U.S. Forest Service.

Other teams of firefighters are called hotshot crews. They hike or travel by truck to the most dangerous parts of the fire. These crews carry all their tools and supplies, including food and water. They can spend days fighting fires and must camp out if necessary. Their backpacks can weigh 110 pounds (49.5 kilograms) or more. Imagine carrying that load while taking a 10-hour hike to a fire!

In areas with good road access, firefighters attack fires with wildland fire engines and use water and foam to fight the fire. When the water is gone, these firefighters can also grab a tool and start "digging a line." Firefighters also use helicopters, pickup trucks, bulldozers, and even boats during the initial attack.

Crews dig trenches and create fire lines from 2 feet to 200 feet (60 centimeters to 61 meters) wide that can run for miles in order to stop a wildfire. They use chain saws, shovels, axes, and other tools to clear away trees, shrubs, grass, and leaf litter that might burn. A fire line is designed to keep a fire from advancing because of a lack of fuel. Firefighters may also start a backfire using a drip torch—a handheld fuel tank—to burn in front of the fire. This eats up potential wildfire fuel, like leaves or dead trees.

Fleets of planes and helicopters fight wildfires. Firefighting planes called air tankers cool wildfires and stop them from spreading. They encircle them with a line of water or fire retardant (a red chemical). Helicopters use

NOW YOU KNOW

Zoologists at the University of Bonn in Germany constructed a forest fire sensor from the example of a small insect—the jewel beetle—that lays its eggs in the wood of freshly burned trees. Believed to be able to detect forest fires from a distance of 50 miles (80 km), the beetle can sense fire and lay its eggs in the smoldering bark of burned trees.

Air tankers can dump up to 2,680 gallons (10,184 liters) of water—enough to fill a small swimming pool—directly onto the flames of a wildfire.

the bull's-eye approach. With a huge bucket dangling from the helicopter, they scoop up water from a nearby lake or river to drop directly onto the fire.

COOL TOOLS

Wildland firefighters need the right

equipment to battle the fires. They wear goggles, gloves, helmets, leather boots, and protective, fire-resistant clothing. Their clothing protects them from the searing heat of flames and does not burn easily. The clothing must also be breathable, cool, and

< TOOLS OF THE TRADE >

Three of the most common tools wildland firefighters use are:

- a Pulaski—a combination ax and digging tool

- a McLeod—a tool that works like a rake and a hoe

- a sharp-edged shovel—used to cut through roots and undergrowth

Carrying too many tools would weigh down the firefighters. The rule of thumb is that firefighters can use only what can be carried without slowing them down. Therefore, each of these tools has many purposes.

lightweight to allow firefighters to dig, chop, shovel, and lug heavy equipment without feeling overly weighed down. Wildland firefighters also carry a fire shelter—a small tent made of reflective material. The shelter can quickly protect a firefighter from the heat and hot gases of a wildfire.

Wildland firefighters may also carry bladder bags, or backpack pumps. These packs are made of high-strength nylon fabric and are fitted with a hand-pumped sprayer. Firefighters lug bags filled with up to 5 gallons (19 L) of water. They spray it on the fuel or litter at the base of the flames in order to put out the fire.

Engine crews are part of the initial attack from back-country roads. The engines carry chain saws, digging tools, and a water pump. Chain saws slice and clear trees. Drip torches spill a burning mixture of diesel fuel and gasoline on materials to burn in a backfire.

Many personal items like earplugs, flares, maps, and compasses are carried into a fire area. Waterproof and windproof thermal space blankets

Approximately 600 firefighters from across the country set up tents in Pomeroy, Washington, in August 2005. They went to combat a 32,000-acre (12,800-hectare) wildfire blazing in the Umatilla National Forest.

shelter firefighters from cold, rain, and wind while they work and sleep.

Even with the proper protection, firefighters still get wet and muddy. Often they must wait days to take a bath or shower. Most of the proteins they store in their packs come from freeze-dried meat, or what some fire-fighters call "mystery meat." Because firefighters work very hard, they are fed big meals at fire camps to keep up their energy. At the camps, each fire-fighter is fed 7,000 calories of food per day. (The average active person needs 2,000 calories per day.)

LOOKOUTS

In the past, people with good vision would climb to the tops of mountains and look all around them for fires every day during the fire season. Sometimes these lookouts would live in a house or cabin by a lookout tower. Lookouts are still used in some parts of the world.

To get a better view of the fire, firefighters climb tall towers—also known as lookouts—and use a tool called a fire finder. The fire finder can swivel 360 degrees to pinpoint smoke on a map. When a lookout locates a fire, he or she communicates the shape, movement, and color of the smoke to help other firefighters determine their next steps. For example, white smoke with a wide base can mean a fire is burning in grass, while a narrow blue or black puffing smoke could mean that thick trees are on fire.

A forest engineer watched for columns of smoke from a fire watchtower in northern Germany after reports of droughts in April 2007.

Chapter 4: *Combating the Fire*

WATCHING THE WEATHER

Because weather affects wildfires significantly, firefighters keep track of weather daily throughout the year. Remote automated weather stations collect information such as wind speed, temperature, and humidity. The weather stations then transmit the information to a command center by radio, cell phone, or satellite. The information is gathered and watched all year long in preparation for possible emergencies.

Relative humidity is a term used to describe how much water vapor is present in the air at a given time. A tool called a sling psychrometer measures relative humidity. The sling psychrometer consists of two thermometers mounted together with a handle attached on a chain. One is a dry-bulb, or regular, thermometer. The other, called a wet-bulb thermometer, has a cloth wick over its bulb.

The wet-bulb wick is first dipped in water, and then the instrument spins. During this process, the water evaporates from the wick, cooling the wet-bulb thermometer. The difference in the temperatures of the wet bulb and the dry bulb determines the relative humidity, or amount of moisture the air can hold. As the air gets drier, more moisture evaporates from the wick, so there is a greater difference between the temperatures of the two thermometers. This means the relative humidity is lower, which causes drier fuels and a greater chance for a fire to spread. Meteorologists have charted these differences for each degree of temperature so that a relative-humidity measurement can be found easily.

Fire behavior analysts determine the safety of a particular fire for firefighters. These experts base their decisions on the data they collect. They carefully study the weather, the topography of the land, and the fuel's effect on the pattern of the fire. They also measure the relative humidity and other weather information. The lower the humidity is, the greater the possibility will be that an extremely dangerous fire will occur.

FOREST SERVICE LAUNCHES WEB-BASED FOREST THREATS VIEWING TOOL

Science Daily
January 2, 2008

The Forest Service's Eastern Forest Environmental Threat Assessment Center (EFETAC) recently launched its forest threats summary viewer, a tool that will provide images, threat distribution maps, additional forestry contact information, and brief descriptions about forest threats throughout the eastern U.S. ...

"The forest threats summary viewer is an excellent tool for individuals concerned about environmental threats to healthy forests, or how these threats affect trees in their backyard," says Danny C. Lee, EFETAC director. "The viewer will make forest research more relevant and useful to forest land managers and homeowners by connecting them with resources to help address their concerns."

High-tech tools such as the forest threat assessment take a Web-based approach to managing a potential fire before it begins. Specific threats like the possible loss of open space, insects, and the spread of diseases are labeled. The user of the tool gets the most current and accurate Web links to federal, state, and local help that offer further information. A tool like this will assist forest landowners, managers, policy-makers, scientists, and the general public to make good decisions about protecting the land and preventing forest fires.

Michael Hutt, the associate direc-

A Doppler on Wheels mobile radar unit monitored a wildfire in western Montana. The radar unit was set up across a river from the fire for protection.

tor of the Rocky Mountain Geo-graphic Science Center at the U.S. Geological Survey in Colorado, and his team are designing a one-of-a-kind computer modeling prediction project. They are studying Grand County in Colorado, hoping to answer several questions. For example, what if a fire breaks out on a particular slope? How many houses are within 1 mile (1.6 km)? Which evacuation routes should people take based on the fire's movement, the weather, and other variables?

To help develop the model, the U.S Forest Service supplied data on soil moisture. The Civil Air Patrol (part of the Air Force) sent pictures from its training flights and ash samples from California's 2007 fires for use in this background research. This will help determine Grand County's expected ash composition from fire. Looking at the ash composition will help pre-dict environmental problems if a fire occurred.

Foresters and geographers are mapping the locations where the most destructive fires are likely to start. To make their maps, they combine data about where fires may start with the conditions that allow fires to spread. For example, a dangerous area would be a heavily wooded forest that has gone through a long dry period. Their work has shown the areas where lim-ited resources can be most effective in stopping the most potentially damag-ing forest fires from ever starting.

SATELLITES

Satellites monitor many of the activi-ties that happen on Earth, and they help firefighters monitor and manage wildfires, too. The Wildland Fire Haz-ard Team has determined what would be necessary for space observations in fire management. A research study was conducted by a group of profes-sionals from all over the world. Many of these professionals had experience with sensors. They wanted to under-stand how to keep track of fire without being directly in or near the fire itself.

The team identified major fac-tors that can improve wildland fire

A color-enhanced image from the National Oceanic and Atmospheric Administration shows areas of heat (red) and smoke (light blue) during a wildfire in Quebec, Canada.

management programs. Earth observation satellites were recommended. They looked at various characteristics needed in various phases of fire management and geographical areas. These requirements included fuel mapping, risk predictions, detection of fire, monitoring, mapping, burned area recovery, and smoke management.

A WILDFIRE EQUATION

Mathematicians are building a model for wildfire movement. These research mathematicians are predicting what a fire will do based upon a model that combines weather and fire patterns. "Fire is very unpredictable," said Jan Mandel, the lead investigator for the project and a mathematician at the University of Colorado's Denver campus. "It can go this way; it can go that way; that's just the nature of the beast." The goal of the research is to figure out probabilities that will help firefighters plan their strategies. The resulting data will indicate likely situations as well as other scenarios that are less likely, but still possible.

Janice Coen, a meteorologist at the National Center for Atmospheric Research in Boulder, Colorado, is one of the model's developers. According to Coen, the model is helping to show why a fire can change its intensity. Her hope is that if the model helps to prevent a mistake or two in fighting a fire, the project would be well worth it.

To make this mathematical model effective, the experts are creating ways to update information every half hour with the most recent fire and weather data. One method is to gather data from planes flying above a fire. The planes contain thermal and infrared sensors that can "see through" the smoke and clouds to find hot spots or areas of intense heat within the fire. They are building software that can automatically process this information directly from the sensors.

In addition, they are developing fire detectors designed to be dropped into the area from airplanes or carried in by firefighters. The detectors will be equipped with radio transmitters, global positioning systems (GPS), and a variety of sensors for measuring smoke, carbon monoxide, temperature, or humidity. The team is designing the devices so fire can

NOW YOU KNOW

In September 1998, a C-130 transport—a plane owned by the National Science Foundation— was outfitted with high-tech equipment by the National Center for Atmospheric Research in Boulder, Colorado. The C-130's mission was to fly over a series of forest fires in the western United States and collect data.

A fire engineer took GPS readings from several areas that had burned in a wildfire.

burn right over them without damaging them. The air and ground sensors would send data to a supercomputer in a remote location from the fire. They would also send continually updated weather information to calculate the direction of the fire and how quickly it is likely to spread. Results would go to handheld computers that firefighters carry with them into the field.

VIRTUAL REALITY

University of Central Florida (UCF) researchers are studying whether interactive simulations of wildfires can push homeowners to invest in insurance to protect against wildfires. The UCF research team is developing an interactive simulation of a wildfire spreading through Volusia County, Florida. The forest or wildfire simulation will be able to show rapidly moving wildfires. This will give participants a realistic look at forests before, during, and after fires and prescribed burns. Participants in the study will decide how much they want to invest in insurance. Their decisions will be compared with those who only receive written information about the danger of wildfires.

Charles Hughes, one of the researchers on this project, said he sees a future for these types of simulations in museums, classrooms, and other places. This is because the cost of the technology required

NOW YOU KNOW

The Crown Fire Initiation and Spread (CFIS) is a software tool that simulates crown fire behavior. The software shows how likely a crown fire is to start, the type of crown fire it is, whether it is active or passive, and its rate of spread.

has dropped in recent years. Picture yourself walking through a forest on a path. Then you turn around and walk back the same way. You'll walk through the same trees and see the same things as on your way in. Everything seen along the path is realistic based on facts gathered from that area, such as the roads, shrubs, and the weather. Then there is a simulated fire, and the path, speed, and intensity of the fire can be predicted by using all of this information.

THE REALITY

Like any other natural disaster, a wildfire can directly affect your home or surrounding areas. Experiencing a dangerous wildfire can be devastating to families and communities. Wildfires sometimes force people to move from their homes.

After a wildfire ends, the disaster affects the survivors for months or even years. For the survivors to rebuild their lives, they must work with several agencies. For example, insurance agencies assess the damage from the wildfire, and contractors work to either build new homes or fix the damaged buildings.

In response to wildfires, the Red Cross provides shelter, food, and health services to families. The Federal Emergency Management Agency works with people and other agencies such as the Red Cross after disasters. They are part of the nation's emergency management system. The Salvation Army provides counseling, food, shelter, and financial assistance to families who have experienced a disaster such as a wildfire.

In 2007, Red Cross personnel prepared to aid victims of a devastating wildfire in Peloponnese, a peninsula in southern Greece.

FACING FIRE

Many federal agencies are involved in fighting wildfires. The major agencies in the Department of the Interior are the Bureau of Land Management, the National Park Service, the Fish and Wildlife Service, and the Bureau of Indian Affairs. These four agencies, along with the Forest Service in the Department of Agriculture, are modifying their policies to include managing fires as a natural occurrence in certain areas and suppressing fires in other areas. All five agencies develop fire management plans that describe which approach will be used and how it will be used.

Over the last several years, federal, state, and local land management agencies have been working with Congress to make important changes in responding to wildfires. Foresters and ecologists

The fire captain of the Monterey County fire strike team briefed his team members about the strategy to contain a wildfire in Big Sur, California.

know we cannot stop all fires from burning, but they believe we may have some effect on how they burn. Some options include thinning small to mid-size trees that can create a "fire ladder" to the forest canopy, prescribing burns, and allowing natural fires to burn under close supervision.

Many still consider thinning helpful where the undergrowth is too thick to burn naturally. The important role of fire in ecology is generally recognized. Using fire effectively will reduce the long-term risk of powerful wildfires and will be the only way to restore and sustain wildlands.

The main obstacle to this method is that the public is against smoke—from the natural fires that park officials monitor and from prescribed burns. Both generate so much criticism that officials are often forced to put them out. While research shows that prescribed burns are a good

Thinning out areas of trees in a forest may slow the spread of wildfires.

approach to protecting against wildfire disasters, thinning the growth is another good option.

Scientists know the hardest decisions ahead are not only scientific, but also social and political. This is because people are involved, and many more people are moving into underdeveloped wildland areas where wildfires are likely to occur. Fire research, technology, resources, and management have become more important than ever in controlling future disasters. ◢

Timeline

1871
More than 1,200 people die and 4 million acres (1.6 million hectares) are burned during a wildfire in Peshtigo, Wisconsin

1910
A huge wildfire in northern Idaho and Montana, driven by hurricane-force winds and called "The Big Blowup," burns 3 million acres (1.2 million hectares) and kills 85 people

1911
Forester William Osborne invents the fire finder used in lookout towers to discover fires that are miles away

1920
Ed Pulaski invents the Pulaski, a combination hoe and ax that became a standard fire tool

1935
The U.S. Forest Service establishes the rule to extinguish all fires by 10 A.M. the day after they start

1940
Smoke jumping—parachuting into a fire as a method of firefighting—is first used to fight wildfires

1942
The first all-female forest firefighting crew in California is assembled

1968
The National Park Service becomes the first federal land management agency to recognize the ways fire can help maintain the landscape

1988
One of the worst wildfires in U.S. history occurs in Yellowstone National Park, Wyoming; about 1.4 million acres (560,000 hectares) of land are burned

2000
The Cerro Grande, New Mexico, fire, which originally began as a prescribed burn, results in the destruction of 235 structures

2002
NASA unveils a new "Natural Hazards" Web site that publishes satellite images of natural hazards around the world

2007
Powerful Santa Ana winds fuel more than 10 large wildfires stretching from Santa Barbara to San Diego in California; the fires destroy more than 2,500 structures and burn 368,969 acres (147,588 hectares) of land

2008
The U.S. Forest Service launches a Web-based tool that shows forest fire threats; two wildfires in Los Angeles burn about 18,000 acres (7,200 hectares) and kill two people

GLOSSARY

air tankers
firefighting planes that spread water and fire retardant on fires to keep them from spreading

backfire
fire purposely ignited in front of a wildfire to consume fuel; it is a way for firefighters to slow the spread of the wildfire

bladder bag
collapsible pack that is made of high-strength nylon fabric and used to spray water on a fire

combustion
process of burning

conduction
transfer of heat through solid material

convection
transfer of heat by the flow of a gas or liquid

crown fire
fire that spreads rapidly and jumps along the canopy of the forest trees

drip torch
handheld fuel tank that is a tool firefighters use to pour a burning mixture of diesel fuel and gasoline on materials to burn in a backfire

fire retardant
chemical that firefighters spread from air tankers in order to keep a wildfire from spreading

ground fire
fire that burns on or below the forest floor

lookout
person who locates fires from tall towers or mountaintops with 360-degree views

McLeod
firefighting tool that works like a rake and a hoe

Pulaski
firefighting tool that is a combination ax and digging tool

radiation
transfer of heat through the electromagnetic spectrum

smoke jumpers
firefighters who jump from an airplane to a wildfire when it is located far from people, highways, and roads

surface fire
fire that burns slowly along the forest floor

FURTHER RESOURCES

ON THE WEB

For more information on this topic, use FactHound.

1. Go to *www.facthound.com*
2. Choose your grade level.
3. Begin your search.

This book's ID number is 9780756540647

FactHound will find the best sites for you.

FURTHER READING

Rothman, Hal. *Blazing Heritage: A History of Wildland Fire in the National Parks.* New York: Oxford University Press, 2007.

Morrison, Taylor. *Wildfire.* Boston: Houghton Mifflin, 2006.

Ring, Susan. *Wildfires.* Philadelphia: Chelsea House, 2003.

Trammel, Howard. *Wildfire.* New York: Children's Press, 2009.

LOOK FOR OTHER BOOKS IN THIS SERIES:

Climate Crisis: The Science of Global Warming

Collapse!: The Science of Structural Engineering Failures

Cure Quest: The Science of Stem Cell Research

Feel the G's: The Science of Gravity and G-Forces

Goodbye, Gasoline: The Science of Fuel Cells

Great Shakes: The Science of Earthquakes

Orbiting Eyes: The Science of Artificial Satellites

Rise of the Thinking Machines: The Science of Robots

Storm Surge: The Science of Hurricanes

SOURCE NOTES

Chapter 1: "The Age of Mega-Fires." CBS News. 30 Dec. 2007. 8 Oct. 2008. www.cbsnews.com/stories/2007/10/18/60minutes/main3380176.shtml

Chapter 2: C. J. Fotheringham, Jon E. Keeley, and Philip W. Rundel. "Blazed and Confused." *The New York Times*. 3 Nov. 2007. 8 Oct. 2008. www.nytimes.com/2007/11/03/opinion/03fotheringham.html?_r=1&scp=1&sq=blazed%20and%20confused&st=cse&oref=slogin

Chapter 3: "Wildfires Leave Behind More Than Ashes." *Science Daily*. 8 Oct. 2007. 8 Oct. 2008. www.sciencedaily.com/releases/2007/10/071003131101.htm

Chapter 4: "Arson Fires Force Hundreds of Hawaiians to Flee." MSNBC 28 Oct. 2007. 8 Oct. 2008. www.msnbc.msn.com/id/21519774/

Chapter 5: "Forest Service Launches Web-based Forest Threats Viewing Tool." *Science Daily*. 2 Jan. 2008. 8 Oct. 2008. www.sciencedaily.com/releases/2007/12/071218113501.htm

ABOUT THE AUTHOR

Lyn Sirota is an active member of the local and national Society of Children's Book Writers and Illustrators. As a graduate of the Institute of Children's Literature, she was accepted into its advanced writing program. Lyn resides in central New Jersey with her husband and two children.

INDEX

aircraft, 27, 28–29, 38
air mass, 15–16
arsenic, 20, 21
arson, 26
ash, 20, 21, 24, 36
aspect, 17–18
automated weather stations, 33

backfires, 25, 28, 30
bladder bags, 30
Bureau of Indian Affairs, 42
Bureau of Land Management, 42

C-130 transport planes, 38
carbon dioxide, 9, 21, 22
carbon monoxide, 38
causes, 10–11, 12, 14, 16
chemical reactions, 6, 9, 13
Civil Air Patrol, 36
clothing, 29–30
Coen, Janice, 38
combustion, 6, 8
computer modeling, 36, 37–38
conduction, 7, 8
controlled burns. See prescribed
    burns.
convection, 7, 8
Crown Fire Initiation and
    Spread (CFIS), 40
crown fires, 11, 12, 17, 18, 40

damage, 4, 5–6, 7, 8, 11, 14, 19,
    22, 40–41
dead fuels, 8–9, 16, 24–25
Department of Agriculture, 42
Department of the Interior, 42
drip torches, 28, 30
dry-bulb thermometers, 33

Eastern Forest Environmental
    Threat Assessment Center
    (EFETAC), 34
ecosystems, 22–23, 25
elevation, 17, 18
engine crews, 30
extended attack fires, 27

farming, 23
Federal Emergency Manage-
    ment Agency, 41

fire behavior analysts, 33
firebrands, 12
fire engines, 28, 30
firefighters, 6, 16, 18, 25, 27–29,
    29–31, 32, 33, 36, 38, 39
firefighting tools, 29–31
firefinders, 32
fire seasons, 10, 13, 32
fire shelters, 30
fire whirls, 15
Fish and Wildlife Service, 42
food, 9, 23, 28, 31, 41
fuels, 6, 7, 8–9, 10, 11, 13, 15,
    16–17, 24–25, 28, 30, 33, 37

global positioning systems
    (GPS), 38
global warming, 13, 21
Great Chicago Fire, 8
ground fires, 11–12, 18

heat transfers, 6–8
helicopters, 28–29
Hosaka, Duane, 26
hotshot crews, 28
Hughes, Charles, 40
humidity, 15, 16, 17, 33, 38
Hutt, Michael, 35–36

insects, 25, 28, 35
insurance, 39, 40–41

jewel beetles, 28

kindling, 17
Kirkland's warbler, 23

lead, 20, 21
Lee, Danny C., 34
lightning strikes, 10
lookouts, 32

Mandel, Jan, 37–38
mapping, 36, 37
McLeod tool, 30
National Center for Atmo-
    spheric Research, 21, 38
National Park Service, 42
National Science Foundation, 38
Native Americans, 23

oxygen, 6, 9, 15

pine beetles, 25
plants, 8, 9, 12–13, 17–18, 21, 22,
    23, 24–25
pollution, 19, 20–22
predictions, 18, 36, 37
prescribed burns, 23–24, 40, 43
prevention, 25, 35, 38, 43
Pulaski tool, 30
pyrocumulus clouds, 13

radiation, 7–8
Red Cross, 41
Rocky Mountain Geographic
    Science Center, 36

Salvation Army, 41
satellites, 33, 36–37
sensors, 28, 36, 38–39
shovels, 28, 30
shrubs, 5, 6, 11, 12, 13, 25, 28, 40
simulations, 39–40
sling psychrometers, 33
slope, 17–18, 36
smoke, 9, 13, 21–22, 32, 37, 38, 43
smoke jumpers, 27
sparks, 11, 15
surface fires, 11, 12

temperatures, 13, 15–17, 22, 33, 38
thinning, 43
tools, 28, 29–31, 32, 33, 34, 35, 40
topography, 15, 17–18, 33
trees, 4, 5, 6, 9, 11–12, 13, 15, 17,
    18, 21, 24, 25, 28, 30, 32, 34, 43

United States Forest Service, 14,
    22, 25, 34, 36, 42
United States Geological
    Survey, 36
University of Bonn, 28
University of Central Florida, 39
University of Colorado, 21, 38

weather, 8, 33, 36, 37, 38, 39, 40
Weaver, Harold, 22
wet-bulb thermometers, 33
wildland firefighters, 6, 27, 28,
    29–30
Wildland Fire Hazard Team, 36
wind, 8, 12, 13, 14, 15, 31, 33

Yellowstone National Park, 8